Amazing
ACTIVITIES
& THINGS TO DO

LORENZ BOOKS

First published in 2000 by Lorenz Books

Lorenz Books are available for bulk purchase for sales promotion
and for premium use. For details, write or call the sales director,
Lorenz Books, 27 West 20th Street, New York, NY 10011;
(800) 354-9657

Lorenz Books is an imprint of Anness Publishing Inc.

The activities and projects in this book were created by:
Sarah Maxwell—*Tasty Treats*; Steve and Jane Parker—*Stunning Science*;
Michael Purton—*Making Music;* Sally Walton and Stephanie
Donaldson—*Growing Things*

Publisher: Joanna Lorenz
Managing Editor, Children's Books:
Gilly Cameron Cooper
Senior Editor: Nicole Pearson
Editors: Lyn Coutts and Louisa Somerville
Editorial Assistant: Jenni Rainford
Photography: John Freeman, Tim Ridley
Design: Axis Design
Additional design: Caroline Grimshaw

Previously published as part of a larger compendium, *The Really Big Book of
Amazing Things to Make and Do* and *The Outrageously Big Activity, Play
and Project Book*

Printed in Hong Kong/ China

10 9 8 7 6 5 4 3 2 1

Foreword

If you fancy being creative, then read on! In this book you'll find great ideas for scrumptious snacks, stunning science experiments and crazy musical instruments, as well as how to grow all kinds of fun, colorful plants. Simple step-by-step recipes show you how to make both sweet and savory treats for a party—or for sharing with a friend. And there's more. You'll be amazed at how easy it is to do science activities and experiments that will truly impress your friends and family. Find out how to make a telephone call that costs nothing and how to hold water upside down in a tumbler! You can also learn how to make musical instruments galore—enough to start your own band, in fact. Or how about growing a giant sunflower, some tasty strawberries or even a chocolate-potted plant that really does smell like chocolate? It's time to roll up your sleeves and let the fun begin. You will be amazed at what's in store for you!

Contents

Tasty Treats

Sarah Maxwell

Introduction

This chapter is full of great ideas and recipes for you to create in your kitchen. Some of the recipes are quite simple to follow. Others will require a bit more concentration for you to get them absolutely right. A few allow you to really get your hands in and get as messy as you like. There are recipes for appetizers and snacks, main meals and lots of ideas for special occasion treats that will really impress your friends. But remember, whether easy or difficult, all the ideas here have been specially designed for you to get lots of fun, pleasure and compliments from your cooking.

One thing is certain, by the time you have tried all the recipes here you will be an expert cook. Family and friends will be forever inviting themselves over to sample your famous cooking.

Whatever you are going to make, there are always a few very important rules to remember before you start. Be safe, be clean and be patient as recipes can easily

turn into disasters if you try to rush things or cut corners to save time.

Always read through the recipe you are planning to make. Write

Peel potatoes with a vegetable peeler.

out a list of what you need, but before you go shopping, check the cupboards to see if there are any ingredients you already have, so you won't have to buy them. It is also a good idea to make a note of how much of a particular ingredient you need, as this will stop you from buying too much and spending too much money. Ask a grown-up to have a quick look through your list before you set off, and always take a grown-up or big brother or sister with you when you go shopping.

While you are cooking, there will be some stages when it will be useful to have a grown-up near by. More important, always ask a grown-up to help with potentially dangerous jobs like transferring food in and out of the oven and on and off the stove top. You will also need help from a grown-up with any stages in the recipe for which you need sharp knives, scissors or electrical equipment, and when anything hot is being handled. Make sure in advance that a grown-up is going to be available if you need them and always get

Always ask a grown-up to hold hot saucepans for you.

Garnish the finished dish to make it look more appetizing.

permission from a grown-up before you start creating your chosen dish in the kitchen.

The recipes here show you, in detailed stages, what you should be doing at each step of the cooking. Just take a look at the children in the pictures and follow what they are doing.

So, when you have read through the rest of the information in the introduction, off you go.

Good luck and have fun!

First Things First

You've chosen your recipe and bought your ingredients, but there are a few simple things to do before you actually start to cook. If there is anything you don't understand, ask a grown-up to explain it to you.

❖ Read through the recipe, from start to finish, very carefully so you have a clear idea of what you are about to be doing and in what order.

❖ Wash and dry your hands. If your hair is long, tie it back. Put on an apron to protect your clothes – plastic ones are best.

❖ Make sure the kitchen surfaces are clean and tidy and you have plenty of space in which to work.

❖ Wash fruit and vegetables before use.

❖ Get all the ingredients you will need sorted out and measured.

Cookie cutters come in all different shapes and sizes and are great for making cookies or cutting out fun sandwich shapes.

Weighing and Measuring

The ingredients in the recipes are measured in ounces (oz) and pints (pt), known as imperial measures. You will also see tsp for teaspoon and tbsp for tablespoon (there are probably a set of special measuring spoons in your kitchen to help you weigh these small amounts).

It is very important to measure carefully and follow recipes exactly. Tasty finished dishes depend on it.

If you want to cook a particular recipe in this book, but you want to make it for more or less people, you can increase or reduce the quantities of ingredients to suit you. If you need help with the multiplication or division, ask a grown-up to help you out.

Why Things Go Wrong

If you find that things are not turning out as they should, then make sure you are following this list of handy tips.

❖ Don't rush.

❖ Do read the recipe through before you start, and follow the instructions and pictures closely.

❖ Do weigh and measure the ingredients carefully.

❖ Don't have any interruptions or distractions while you are in the kitchen, because this can cause you to forget where you are in the recipe, and leave parts out.

❖ If cooking in the oven, don't keep opening the oven door as this will cause the temperature to drop.

❖ Do make sure you cook things for the proper length of time.

A food processor makes mixing ingredients easy and quick. Always ask a grown-up to help you with this piece of equipment.

To cook successfully, you must always measure your ingredients carefully.

Be Clean and Tidy

When you are cooking and handling food, you must be aware of the bacteria which are all around. Most bacteria are harmless, but it is important to keep the harmful ones away by following a few simple rules.

❖ Always wash your hands before you handle food and keep washing them every now and then while you are cooking, to keep them as clean as possible.

❖ Wear a clean apron and tie long hair back.

❖ Have a clean, damp cloth handy, so you can wipe the surfaces if you make a mess. Don't forget to rinse the cloth when you have used it.

Wash your hands before you start to cook and dry them on a clean dish towel.

❖ Try to tidy up and wash up as you go, so you won't have so much to do at the end.

❖ Wash your chopping board regularly and every time you use it for a new ingredient.

❖ Always wash fruit and vegetables before you use them and clear away any peel.

❖ Have a garbage can near by, so you can keep putting things in it rather than letting the garbage pile up as you cook.

Be Safe in the Kitchen

There are some things in the kitchen which can be very dangerous. Make sure you have a grown-up's permission before you start cooking and ask them to be around to help with the more dangerous stages of cooking. Always read through the recipe to see when and where you might need the help of a grown-up, then follow these basic rules:

❖ Always ask a grown-up to light the oven or stove top – never do it yourself.

❖ Go slowly and carefully in the kitchen – rushing around causes accidents.

❖ Always use potholders or a dish towel when handling hot things. Better still, ask a grown-up to do it for you.

❖ Never leave the kitchen when something is cooking – you don't know what might happen while you're gone!

Always wear an apron to protect your clothes when cooking.

1 Peel the eggs – see handy hints opposite. Cut a thin slice from the side of one of the eggs, and a slice from the pointed end of the other egg.

2 Cut the cherry tomato in half and then cut one half into four pieces to make the egg bug. Cut the big tomato in half for the mushroom.

3 To make a base on the serving dish, arrange the shredded carrot on a plate, spreading it out so that it is flat and even.

4 Peel away strips of cucumber skin and cut two slices to stand on the eggs. You can cut more for decoration.

5 Place the cucumber slices on top of the shredded carrot, then put an egg on top of each one. Don't forget that the egg bug lies down and the mushroom stands up!

6 To finish off the egg bug, use a toothpick stick to put some mayonnaise on the big end and top of the lying-down egg. Stick on half a cherry tomato for the face and two quarters on top for the spikes. Put a blob of mayonnaise on top of the mushroom egg and put a larger tomato half on top.

7 Use the toothpick to put tiny spots of mayonnaise all over the mushroom and to make the eyes, nose and mouth for the egg bug's face. Use sprouts for the egg bug's feet.

Cheese Dip with Dunks

This dish that George is making is great for a party and all your friends will love dunking their favorite chips and vegetables into the rich and creamy dip. Watch out for dunkin' grown-ups, they are bound to want to join in all the fun! If you want to give the strips of vegetables for dunking a crinkled effect, use a crinkle-bladed knife to cut them.

YOU WILL NEED THESE INGREDIENTS
Serves 8–10

8 oz carton of cream cheese

4 tbsp milk

small bunch of fresh chives

1 small carrot, peeled

For dunking: 3 in strips of cucumber, ¹/₂ of a red, orange and yellow bell pepper, seeded and cut into strips, 4 baby sweetcorn, potato or tortilla chips

8–10 cherry tomatoes

Special equipment: scissors

Handy hints:
❖ If you prefer your dips to be less rich tasting, you could use a low-fat cream cheese instead of full-fat cream cheese.
❖ Chives are a fresh herb which look a little like grass and taste of onions. If you can't find any, you can snip the green tops off scallions instead.
❖ You could also add celery, cauliflower florets, carrot sticks, slices of apple and radishes to your selection of dipping vegetables.

1 Spoon the full-fat soft cheese into a mixing bowl and beat it with a wooden spoon until soft and creamy.

2 Add the milk to the cheese, a little at a time. Beat the mixture well each time you pour more milk in.

3 Beat the mixture hard for about 2 minutes. If necessary, add more milk to make the dip runnier.

4 Cut the chives finely and add to the cheese mixture, saving some.

5 Grate the carrot on the smallest holes of the grater. Save some and stir the rest into the cheese mixture.

6 Spoon the mixture into a bowl and sprinkle on the remaining chives and grated carrot. Cut the cucumber, baby sweetcorn and peppers for dunking into thin strips.

7 Place the bowl of dip in the centre of a serving plate and arrange little groups of the strips for dunking around the edges. Add the tomatoes and crisps or tortilla chips and let your guests start dippin' and dunkin'.

Swimming Fish Cakes

There are lots of variations on this recipe that Joshua is making. You could serve the swimming fish on a sea of your favorite vegetable. Try a sea of peas or corn, or a mixture of both. If you particularly like modeling, make lots of tiny fish, and serve everyone with two or more. But remember to tell your grown-up helper that the small fish won't take as long to cook as the bigger ones.

Handy hints:
❖ Ask a grown-up to open the can of tuna with a can opener, as this can be dangerous and you might cut yourself.
❖ You could make the fish cake mixture and even shape the cakes up to several hours in advance, if you like. Keep them in the fridge until you are ready to cook and eat them.

YOU WILL NEED THESE INGREDIENTS
Serves 4

1 oz butter

3 large potatoes

1 egg   dash of milk

7 oz can tuna chunks in water, drained

3 oz fresh breadcrumbs

pepper

oil, for shallow frying

For the garnish: 4 peas

a few sprigs of fresh curly parsley

1/2 cucumber peeled, cut in half lengthwise and very thinly sliced, 4 slices of lemon, 4 thin slices of tomato

Special equipment: vegetable peeler, potato masher, can opener

1 Put the wooden skewers in a shallow dish of cold water. Leave them to soak in the water for about 30 minutes, then remove them and throw away the water.

2 Put the rice and turmeric in a saucepan. Ask a grown-up to cover it with boiling water, simmer for 15 minutes, then drain. Return the rice to the saucepan and cover with a lid.

3 While the rice is cooking, put the peppers on a chopping board and cut out the white seeds and pith inside. Rinse the peppers under cold water and cut them into chunks.

4 Thread the chicken on to the skewers as shown. This will give a coiled effect when it cooks.

5 Thread the other ingredients on to the skewers in whatever order you like. Make sure you finish each one with a piece of baby corn, pushing the skewer only a little way in.

6 Put the kebabs on the broiling pan and drizzle over some of the salad dressing. Ask a grown-up to put the kebabs under a hot broiler for about 5 minutes, then to turn them over and continue broiling for another 5 minutes, until the chicken is cooked.

7 Just before the kebabs are cooked, put some rice on to the serving plates and spread it out.

Arrange the kebabs on the rice and they are ready to serve.

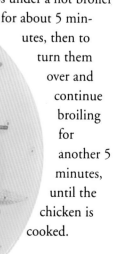

23

Crazy Popcorn

This multi-colored cheese-flavored mixture that Andreas is making will make your party the talk of the town. Have fun choosing your own colors for the popcorn and cheese. If you don't like Saga Blue, use white Cheddar cheese instead. And if you haven't got a large enough container to hold all of the popcorn, or have a lot of guests who are going to want to eat right away, then fill two containers instead.

Handy hints:
❖ You must use powdered food coloring as liquid coloring will turn the popcorn soggy. You will find the powdered kind in cake decorating shops.
❖ You can buy microwave popcorn which is especially for cooking in the microwave. Follow the instructions on the package for cooking (ask a grown-up to operate the microwave) and color it as directed in steps 4–6.

YOU WILL NEED THESE INGREDIENTS
Serves 10–15

1 tbsp vegetable oil

6 oz popcorn kernels

green, red and blue powdered food colorings

2 oz grated Colby cheese

2 oz grated Saga Blue cheese

Special equipment: 3 large plastic bags

1 Put the vegetable oil in a large saucepan. Pour in the popcorn kernels and stir with a wooden spoon to coat them all in the oil.

2 Place the lid on the saucepan and ask a grown-up to heat the popcorn on the stove top, gently, for about 5 minutes, until you hear the popcorn starting to pop. Do not remove the lid.

3 When the popping noises have slowed down and you hardly hear any popping at all, ask the grown-up to put the saucepan on a trivet on the table. You can now remove the lid.

4 Put small amounts of popcorn in each plastic bag. The bags should be see-through so you can see the color of the popcorn changing when you add the color.

5 Use a tiny spoon to add a small amount of food coloring to each of the bags of popcorn. You can choose what colors you use and how much popcorn you want to make a particular color.

6 Close the bag and hold it tightly in one hand. Shake the bag and tap it with the other hand, tossing the popcorn inside the bag to coat it evenly in the coloring. As you color each batch, tip it into a large bowl.

7 When all the popcorn is colored, add the grated cheese.

Wash your hands, then carefully toss the mixture together evenly. Try not to tip it over the sides of the container.

Frozen Banana Pops

These pops are great for a summer party. But if you haven't got any party plans, just make a batch of pops and freeze them all for yourself. They will keep in the freezer, in sealed bags, for about a month. Sophie has coated her pops with coconut, but if you don't like it, choose your own coating. Try toasted, chopped nuts or crumbled chocolate flake bars. They are all delicious!

Handy hints:
❖ You can buy popsicle sticks in most hardware shops and supermarkets, but if you want to be crafty and environmentally friendly collect up your own and your friends' used ones. Wash and dry them and they'll be as good as new!
❖ Don't peel the bananas too early, otherwise they will start to get brown and mushy.

YOU WILL NEED THESE INGREDIENTS
Serves 8

red, blue and green food colorings (powdered or liquid)

4 oz dried shredded coconut

8 small bananas

a little maple syrup

Special equipment: 8 popsicle sticks, pastry brush, baking sheet, plastic wrap

1 Divide the coconut into three small bowls and add a small amount of food coloring to each. Stir well, until the coconut is evenly colored.

2 Pour the red, blue and green colored coconut on to separate plates and spread it out evenly.

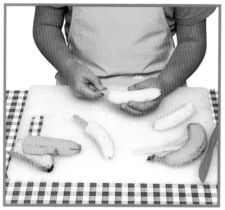

3 Peel the bananas and cut a small piece off one end of each one, to make it straight. Carefully press a popsicle stick into the straight end of each banana, taking care not to push the stick in too far, as it might break through the side.

4 Pour some maple syrup into a bowl. Holding the stick and using a pastry brush, brush an even coating of maple syrup over each banana. Put on a plate when coated.

5 Still holding the popsicle sticks, dip and roll the bananas in the colored coconut until they are coated evenly.

6 Lay the bananas on a baking sheet covered with plastic wrap. The bananas must not touch. Freeze for 4 hours.

Take the banana pops off the baking sheet and arrange on a serving plate. Ideally you should wait about 15 minutes, to let the bananas soften a little before you eat them.

Jello Pond

By molding fondant icing just like play-dough, you can be really creative with this recipe and make your own monsters for a lake or pond scene. Follow what Sophie is doing to see how. Try water snakes, ducks, waterlilies, fish and frogs. Your lake or pond will be even more realistic if you add a drop of green food coloring to the jello while you are dissolving it. When you come to chop up the set jello, do not mix it too much or the jello will turn to liquid again.

Handy hints:

❖ It is a good idea to wear rubber gloves when you are coloring the fondant icing, otherwise your hands will get colored too.

❖ The easiest way to get the color of the icing even is to roll it out into a sausage shape. bring the two ends of the sausage together and start rolling out a new sausage. Keep rolling this way until you are happy with the color.

❖ Put the chopped jello into the 'creature' bowl at the very last minute before serving, as the 'wet' jello will make the fondant creatures start to leak some of their color.

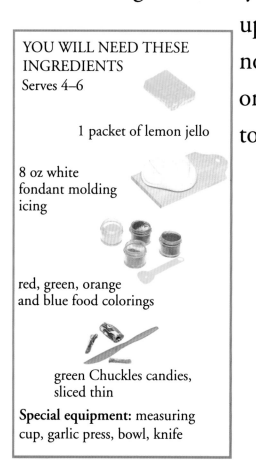

YOU WILL NEED THESE INGREDIENTS
Serves 4–6

1 packet of lemon jello

8 oz white fondant molding icing

red, green, orange and blue food colorings

green Chuckles candies, sliced thin

Special equipment: measuring cup, garlic press, bowl, knife

So scientists usually specialize. This means they study just one or a few subjects. For example, medical scientists study why people get sick, and how to make them better. Biologists study animals and plants, where they live and how they grow. Chemists study chemicals and other substances, what they are made of, and how they can be changed and used. Physicists study how things move, what holds them together or pulls them apart, and how energy makes things happen. Astronomers study the planets, stars, the sun and moon, and the whole universe.

How to Do an Experiment

Whatever scientists study, they usually work in the same way. This is called the scientific method. They do not rush, and they always keep things clean and safe.

• First, the scientist finds out as much as possible about the subject. This is called research. What is already known about the subject? What experiments have other scientists done, and what did they discover? Do people really know the facts, or are they just guessing?

• Then the scientist decides on a good question to ask. It should be a new question that no one has asked before. But it must not be too complicated. Most scientists find out more by working in small stages, bit by bit.

• The scientist may have an idea of the possible answer to the question. In other words, he or she may guess what will happen in the experiment. This possible answer to the question is called a theory.

• Next, the scientist thinks of an experiment that will test the theory to find the answer to the question. This is called planning or designing the experiment. In a good experiment, everything happens clearly and safely, and nothing can go wrong – hopefully!

• Now, the scientist gathers all the bits and pieces to do the experiment. These are called the materials and equipment. Everything is set out neatly and cleanly, and labeled clearly, so that there are no mix-ups.

• At last, the scientist carries out the experiment, working carefully and safely. He or she finds out what

happens by looking and listening, and perhaps, by feeling or smelling. The things that happen are called the results. These are written down carefully in the Science Record Book. Everything is cleaned up and put away afterward.

• Next, the scientist thinks about the results. Were they expected, or not? Is the theory right, or wrong? If the theory is right, the scientist has found something new. If the theory is wrong, the scientist can try to think of another theory, or perhaps, the experiment did not work properly. Remember, no experiment is a failure. A good scientist can always learn from the results, whatever they are.

• After more experiments, the scientist will be able to gather the answers together. He or she must check everything, then check it again. Finally, the scientist may make a new discovery and become famous.

Being a Good Scientist

Scientists are very careful people. They have to be. They often work with dangerous machines, equipment and chemicals. And science can be very costly. So scientists also need to be sure that their experiments are worthwhile, and that there will be no mistakes. So they make sure everything is thought out and prepared carefully.

When you do experiments, get the materials and equipment ready first. Have a clean, safe area where you do your experiments, as described over the page. And ask a grown-up to check that everything is safe.

Water is great fun to splash around, as long as you are working in a waterproof area.
Science tip For experiments with water or other liquids, see if you can do them in a large bowl, such as a mixing bowl. This catches any splashes or spills.

Heat can be very dangerous. Hot water and steam can burn or scald your skin. And when very hot water is poured into cold jars, beakers or bowls, it can make them crack or melt. So *always* get a grown-up to help you with experiments that need hot water and make sure your equipment can stand up to it. Cookers and kettles must only be used when a grown-up is present. Liquids can boil over suddenly, and things may catch fire without warning.

Use a pitcher and a funnel when pouring liquids.

Never touch electric sockets, plugs or wires.

Wear a pair of rubber gloves when handling vinegar or lemon juice.

Always ask a grown-up to cut anything with sharp scissors or a craft knife.

Science tip Put a metal teaspoon into a jar before pouring in hot water. This should stop the heat from cracking the jar.

Ice can freeze skin just as badly as hot water can burn. Ice has the added danger that it sticks to dry skin. When you make ice in a freezer, get a grown-up to help you.
Science tip Use rubber or dishwashing gloves when handling ice. Wet the ice and the gloves first, so they do not stick together.

Electricity from a small battery is usually safe, since there is not enough power to give a shock. Static electricity can sometimes be felt as a tingle that makes you jump. For example, when it builds up on a car and you touch the handle. But the static that builds up on a balloon, as shown in one of the experiments, is too small to feel.
Science tip The electricity that is used in the home is very dangerous. It can kill! NEVER touch electric sockets, plugs or wires.

Chemicals used here are mostly substances used for cooking, and they are harmless in normal quantities. But

Put a metal teaspoon into a jar before pouring in hot water.

good scientists know that chemicals can be dangerous if they get into the wrong place. This includes near too much heat or inside your body if you swallow them. Never taste or eat chemicals that you are using for experiments. Always ask a grown-up to get the things you need from the kitchen cabinet. *Never* touch cleaning chemicals, medicines or alcohol.

Science tip Use rubber gloves to handle large quantities of acids like vinegar or lemon juice.

Cutting
and making holes can be quite difficult. Scissors and sharp points can be dangerous if they are not used properly. So ask a grown-up to help.

Science tip Draw a line where you are going to cut with scissors, before you start cutting. It is usually easier to follow a drawn line.

Label everything.
It is the sign of a good scientist. Your experiment might be ruined if you cannot remember what you put in each jar or if you get your chemicals mixed up. Write labels on pieces of paper or use special sticky-backed labels. Stick these in the right place, or put them under jars or beakers.

Science tip Use a pencil for your labels. Some felt-tipped pens can blot and run if splashed with water.

Your Science Record Book

All scientists record their experiments and the results. You need to know exactly what you did during an experiment so that you can repeat it to check the result or change it to find out something else. Each time you do an experiment, record the following information in your book. If you find writing difficult, ask a grown-up to help with some of the details and draw a picture of what happened, instead.

• the day and date
• the experiment's name and the idea behind it
• how you did your experiment, perhaps with a drawing or diagram
• the results, written in words, or perhaps as a chart with check marks and crosses

You can make a Science Record Book by covering a notebook or school-type exercise book with colored paper. The paper needs to be about $1\frac{1}{4}$–$1\frac{1}{2}$ in larger all around than the book when it is opened flat.

Further Research

When scientists have finished their set of experiments, they often try to find out a little more, perhaps by changing the experiment slightly. See if you can make changes to some of your experiments to find out more. Record what you do and your results in your Science Record Book.

Your Science Record Book

1 Place the book centered on the colored paper, with one cover open. Turn the edges of the paper over the cover, and paste them down with glue. You can snip the corners of the paper to give a neater finish. Repeat with the other cover.

2 Decorate the cover with something scientific, perhaps numbers, drawings of test-tubes and scientific equipment, or cutout photographs of scientific gadgets.

3 Record all the information that you have learned from your experiments. If you like, you can stick some of the things you have made in the book, to keep.

Where to Do Experiments

Many scientists work in special rooms called laboratories. There, they have all the equipment, materials, tools and machines they need to do their experiments. But not all science happens in laboratories. To do research, many scientists go to libraries to read books. They visit exhibitions and museums to find out more. They also meet other scientists and talk about their work.

The Home Laboratory

You can set up your own laboratory in your home or school. It might be in a kitchen, bathroom, shed or garage. You usually need somewhere with waterproof surfaces, where there is no danger of damaging furniture or carpets. Ask a grown-up to choose the best place.

The main thing you will need is a large work surface, like a table. The place should be brightly lit and not too hot or cold. For some experiments, you will need a freezer or a refrigerator with a freezing compartment. You will sometimes need lots of water. Warm water can come from a faucet or a kettle. You might also need somewhere to heat up a saucepan. Always ask a grown-up to help.

Science tip Cover your work surface with several layers of old newspaper. This stops paint and food coloring from staining the work surface and will also absorb spilled liquids and glue.

Materials and Equipment

You will find most of the materials, equipment and tools that you need for your experiments around the house. Always gather everything you need, and check it before you start the experiment. If you do not, you may run out of something halfway through.

If necessary, you can buy extra supplies of pencils, pens, scissors, sticky tape, paper, cardboard, blotting paper, glue, sticky labels and shapes, poster paints and similar things from a good stationery store or office suppliers.

You can find food colorings, baking soda, vinegar, lemon juice, milk, spoons, toothpicks, skewers and similar things in the kitchen.

Batteries, wires and small flashlight bulbs are sold in hardware stores or hobby shops. You can buy small mirrors from a drugstore and sand or gravel from a home-improvement store.

Be a Green Scientist

Good scientists know that they must look after our planet by saving resources, recycling things and not damaging the environment or causing waste and pollution. This is called being "green" since it helps to save trees, plants, flowers, animals and natural places on our planet Earth.

You can be a "green scientist" by saving, reusing and recycling things. You will also save money!

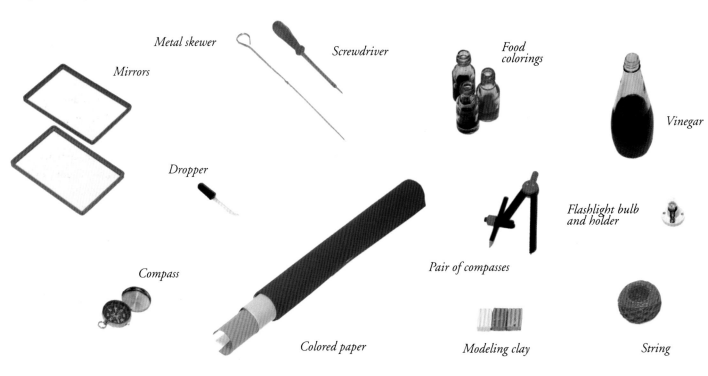

Metal skewer   *Screwdriver*   *Food colorings*

Mirrors   *Vinegar*

Dropper   *Flashlight bulb and holder*

Compass   *Pair of compasses*

Colored paper   *Modeling clay*   *String*

1 Decorate the battery to make it look powerful by winding a piece of wide colored sticky tape around it.

2 Cut out some zigzag "lightning flashes" from the yellow cardboard and stick them on to the sides of the battery with glue.

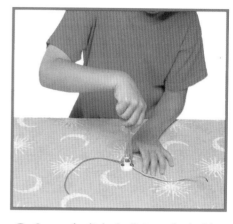

3 Screw the light bulb into the holder. Push the end of a piece of wire under one of the connecting screws. Screw it down. Repeat with another piece of wire under the other screw.

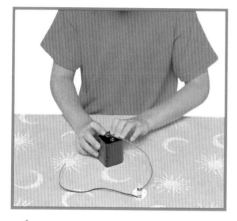

4 Take the end of one of these pieces of wire and twist it on to one of the battery terminals (the bits of metal on the top of the battery).

5 Twist the end of the third piece of wire on to the other battery terminal. Make sure that both these wires grip the terminals tightly.

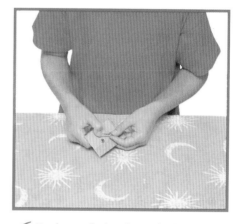

6 Push two holes through the piece of cardboard, the length of the paper clip apart. Push a split pin through one hole. Push the other split pin through the paper clip and then through the other hole. Open the ends of the pins under the card.

7 Twist one free wire end around one split pin and the other around the other split pin. When the paper clip touches both split pins, the switch is ON (green dot) and the light bulb shines. When the paper clip is moved away from the split pin, the switch is OFF (red dot).

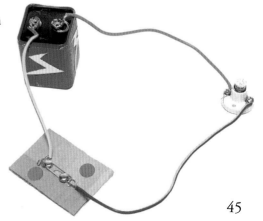

Tumbler Telephone

Can you talk to a friend quietly, when he or she is at the other end of a big room? Liam's telephone works by sending the sound waves of his voice along the string. They go along the string as very fast to-and-fro movements called vibrations. When Liam talks into the tumbler or cup, the sound waves hit the bottom of the tumbler and make it vibrate. The vibrations pass along the string to the tumbler at the other end. They shake the bottom of this tumbler, which makes sound waves that go into Lorenzo's ear.

Traveling waves

Sound waves travel well through air. They go through lots of other things too, such as water, wood, metals and glass. In fact, sound travels much faster and further as vibrations in water, metal and glass than it does through air. This is why whales and dolphins can "talk" to each other across huge distances in the ocean.

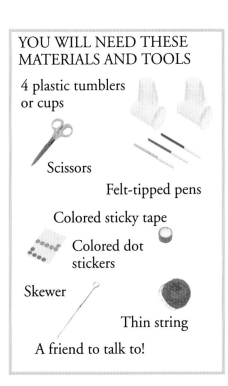

YOU WILL NEED THESE MATERIALS AND TOOLS

4 plastic tumblers or cups

Scissors

Felt-tipped pens

Colored sticky tape

Colored dot stickers

Skewer

Thin string

A friend to talk to!

With his own tumbler telephone, Liam never gets a wrong number, and the lines are never busy. Also, his calls are always free!

!The tumbler telephone works well if the string is stretched tight and straight, and nothing touches it. Otherwise the vibrations cannot travel along it properly. The tumblers should be held by their rims only, so the bottoms are free to vibrate. Children may need help with cutting the tumblers and making holes with a sharp point.

1 Carefully cut the bottoms off two of the tumblers about ¾ in from the base. You may need to ask a grown-up to help you with this.

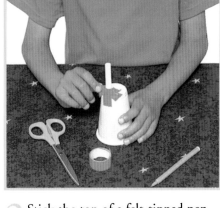

2 Stick the top of a felt-tipped pen to the bottom of each of the other two tumblers. These will be the "antennas."

3 Ask a grown-up to cut small holes in the cut-off tumbler bottoms. Slip them neatly over the "antennas" to hold them in place.

4 Tape the cut-off bottoms in place. Add more strips of sticky tape for decoration.

5 Make a "key pad" on each telephone with colored dot stickers. Write numbers on the dots.

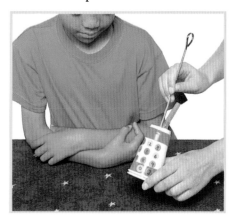

6 Ask a grown-up to make a tiny hole in the bottoms of the tumblers with a skewer.

7 Thread the ends of the string through the holes in the telephones. Tie a large knot in each end of the string.

Chatting on the Telephone

Your friend walks away with one of the tumbler telephones, until the string is stretched tight, and holds the telephone to his or her ear. You speak into the telephone, and your friend listens. When you have finished talking, say "Over" like a real walkie-talkie user. Hold the telephone to your ear to hear your friend's reply. Try using longer string to see if the telephone still works. Measure the greatest length, and write the results in your Science Record Book.

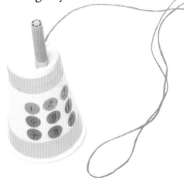

Hold Water Upside Down!

This famous trick looks impossible, or perhaps it is magic. Can you really hold water in an upside-down tumbler? Yes. Antonino shows that it truly does work. It depends on science. The force that pulls you, a cat, a chair and everything else in the world, down toward the ground is called gravity. Gravity tries to make the water fall out of the upside-down tumbler toward the ground. But in this trick, air keeps the water in the tumbler.

Heavy air

Air has weight, although it does not weigh much. There is a lot of it pressing on us, since there is a huge amount of air high above. We do not notice this pressing force, because we are used to it. It is called **air pressure**, and it is this that keeps the water in the glass. The water is trapped inside the glass by the cardboard. Air presses down, around and up underneath the cardboard, holding it in place and keeping the water inside the tumbler.

YOU WILL NEED THESE MATERIALS AND TOOLS

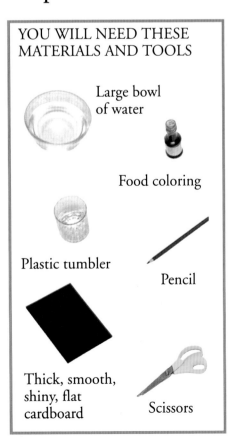

Large bowl of water

Food coloring

Plastic tumbler

Pencil

Thick, smooth, shiny, flat cardboard

Scissors

This experiment involves a lot of water and does not always work right the first time. So it should be performed in a suitable waterproof area. Use a plastic tumbler and bowl rather than glass ones, for safety. We have used glass ones here so you can see how the experiment works. Clean, smooth, shiny, flat cardboard is best. The experiment does not work as well if the cardboard becomes soggy or bent.

Antonino is using the science of air, water and gravity to stop his feet from getting wet!

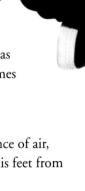

1 Add a little food coloring to the water in the bowl, and stir it around. This is so you can see the water inside the tumbler.

2 Draw around the rim of the tumbler on to the cardboard. Then draw a square around this circle, about ³/₄ in larger than the circle all around.

3 Carefully cut out the square of cardboard. It should fit easily over the top of the tumbler, with plenty of extra around the rim.

4 Put the tumbler into the bowl of water. Hold it under, with the open end pointing up. Make sure that it fills up completely.

5 Make sure there are no bubbles of air inside the tumbler, by tapping it. The trick will not work if there is any air in the tumbler.

6 Turn the tumbler upside down. Lift it partly out, but keep the rim under the water. Slide the cardboard into the water and under the rim.

7 Hold the cardboard firmly against the rim of the tumbler. Slowly lift the cardboard and tumbler, still upside down, out of the water.

8 Hold the tumbler upside down and level. Without sliding the cardboard, take your other hand away from the cardboard.

Air, Water and Weather

The layer of air all around the Earth is called the **atmosphere**. Air's weight changes when it gets hot or cold, and these changes cause our weather. When air is warmed by the sun, it rises higher. Cooler air moves along to take its place. This is wind. As air rises, the invisible moisture in it turns to tiny drops of water. These make clouds. As the drops get bigger, they fall as rain.

The Great Iceberg Puzzle

One of the great puzzles of nature is how icebergs float. Icebergs are huge lumps of ice that drift about in the cold seas near the North and South Poles. Some icebergs are bigger than cities. They weigh thousands of tons. As water gets colder, it gets heavier. So cold water sinks below warm water. Icebergs are frozen water and so are even colder. So why do they not sink to the bottom of the sea? Lorenzo finds out why in this experiment by using tiny icebergs from a refrigerator or freezer. They will work the same as a real iceberg, but they are much smaller!

Lorenzo has made lots of colored "icebergs." He is investigating how they float and then melt.

50

YOU WILL NEED THESE MATERIALS AND TOOLS

A large see-through bowl of warm water

Ice-cube tray

Food colorings

Pitcher

Plastic paint pots or jars

Spoon

Light ice

As water gets colder, it becomes heavier. But this only happens down to the temperature of 4°C (40°F). If it gets colder than that, it begins to get lighter again and so rises toward the surface. When it cools to 0°C (32°F), liquid water freezes into solid ice. This cold ice is light, and it floats on water. This means that animals and plants which live in water do not have to freeze solid themselves when the temperature drops to or below freezing. They can survive in the cold water below the ice that floats on ponds and lakes.

1 Make some mini-icebergs by putting food coloring into some water in paint pots or jars. You can make them in several different colors, but do not mix the colors together.

2 Spoon the colored water carefully into the ice-cube tray or other containers, if you wish. Put these into a freezer. Leave until frozen solid.

3 When the ice cubes are frozen, fill the large bowl with warm water. Ask a grown-up to help you with this. Then remove the ice-cube tray from the freezer or refrigerator.

4 Drop colored ice cubes into the water. Watch what happens. Do they sink? Look at the bowl from the side. Can you see the ice melting? What does it do?

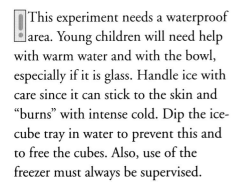

This experiment needs a waterproof area. Young children will need help with warm water and with the bowl, especially if it is glass. Handle ice with care since it can stick to the skin and "burns" with intense cold. Dip the ice-cube tray in water to prevent this and to free the cubes. Also, use of the freezer must always be supervised.

Underwater Fountain

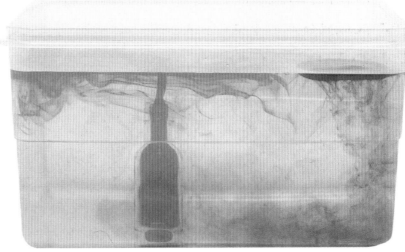

You can investigate how warm water floats and cold water sinks by making an underwater fountain. Fill a large bowl with cold water. Then fill a small plastic bottle with warm water. (The plastic bottle must be small enough to sink below the surface of the water in the bowl.) Add some food coloring to it. Carefully lower the bottle into the bowl, and make it sit on the bottom. Does the warm, colored water stay in the bottle? Where does it go? Draw a picture of your fountain in your Science Research Book to show your results. You could also try dropping some colored ice cubes, made with a contrasting food coloring, into the water. The ice is lighter than the water around it, so it floats. The warmer water melts the colored ice. But the colored water that comes from the ice is colder and heavier than the water around it, so it sinks. Look very carefully to see the cold, colored water trickling from the iceberg and sinking to the bottom.

Kitchen Chemistry

Everything in the world is made of chemicals. Some are artificial chemicals, like those made in factories. Others are natural chemicals, like those in your own body and in the rocks and soil. Even the food you eat is made of chemicals. Scientists who study chemicals are called chemists. You can be a kitchen chemist, like Dean, and study the chemicals in the cabinet. Cooking is a form of chemistry. You mix together the chemicals and make them join together, or react, to form a tasty snack.

The acid test

Some cooking substances, like vinegar or lemon juice, are sour. They are called **acidic**. Other kitchen substances, like baking soda, are slightly slimy and bitter. They are called **basic** or **alkali**. Bases are the opposite of acids. Chemists often need to know whether chemicals are acids or bases. If they do not know what the chemicals are, they should never taste them to find out, because many chemicals are poisonous. So chemists make special substances called **chemical indicators** to test them. Red cabbage water is a good chemical indicator to tell the difference between acids and bases.

Young children must be supervised in the kitchen since some foods and liquids can cause sickness in large quantities. Chopping and boiling the cabbage should always be done by a grown-up.

Dean has put a strip of blotting paper into each of his test jars. The name of the test juice or liquid is marked on the paper in pencil. He can then let the strips dry and clip them into his Science Record Book.

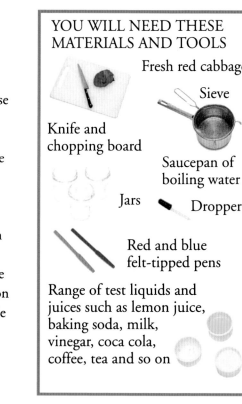

YOU WILL NEED THESE MATERIALS AND TOOLS

Fresh red cabbage

Sieve

Knife and chopping board

Saucepan of boiling water

Jars

Dropper

Red and blue felt-tipped pens

Range of test liquids and juices such as lemon juice, baking soda, milk, vinegar, coca cola, coffee, tea and so on

1 Ask a grown-up to chop the cabbage, put it into boiling water for about 15 minutes, then strain the water through a sieve.

2 While the chemical indicator (the red cabbage water) is cooling, put a little tap water into each jar. Get your Science Record Book ready.

3 Add about 15 drops of the chemical indicator to each jar, using the dropper. Look at the color and note it in your Science Record Book.

4 Add one test liquid to a jar, such as a spoonful of juice squeezed from a lemon. Stir it in. Watch and note down any color change.

5 Add another test liquid, such as a spoonful of milk, to the next jar. As before, mix it, and note down any color change in your book.

6 Add the next test liquid, such as a few drops of vinegar, to the next jar. Note any change. Do this with the other test liquids and juices.

Recording Your Results

Color in the result of each experiment in your Science Record Book. Draw three columns. In the first column, write the name or draw a picture of the test substance. In the second column, put a check mark for those that turned red or orange with a red felt-tipped pen. In the third column, put a check mark for those that turned purple or blue with a blue felt-tipped pen. Acids join or react with the red cabbage water to turn it red or orange. Bases do the same but turn it purple or blue. During the experiment, keep one jar that contains just the chemical indicator. Scientists call this a "control." You can compare the color changes in the other jars with the original color in the "control" jar.

53

Vinegar Volcano

What happens when acids and bases (alkalis) meet? Kirsty has made a peaceful-looking tropical island, but it is about to get shaken by a huge volcano. She can make the volcano explode or erupt using simple chemicals – the acid vinegar and the base bicarbonate of soda. The spectacular effect is caused by the reaction between the acid and the base. The food coloring makes it look like real, red-hot, runny rock.

YOU WILL NEED THESE MATERIALS AND TOOLS

Red food coloring

Vinegar

2 small plastic or glass bottles

Funnel

Baking soda

Large, blue plate

Sand

White glue

Colored paper

Pencil

Scissors

Colored sticky tape

Fizzy gas

Everything is made of chemicals. And all chemicals are made of tiny particles called **atoms**. During a chemical reaction, the groups of atoms are taken apart, mixed and shuffled, then joined together in different groups, to make new chemicals. When vinegar is mixed with baking soda, one of the new chemicals formed is a gas. The bubbles of this gas make the volcano fizz.

This chemical reaction is not dangerous. The gas produced is carbon dioxide, but with the recommended quantities of vinegar and baking soda, its amounts are very small and not harmful. However, the child should be supervised in case of spillage.

Kirsty's volcano is based on a simple chemical reaction. A real volcano is millions of times more powerful and based on heat and pressure.

54

1 Add some red food coloring to some vinegar in a small bottle using the funnel.

2 Wash and dry the funnel. Use it to put 3 or 4 teaspoons of baking soda into another small bottle.

3 Stand this bottle in the middle of the plate as the volcano. Pile the sand around it.

4 Paint the sides of the bottle with glue, to make the sand stick. Leave the bottle's mouth clear. This is the volcano's opening or crater.

5 Make a palm tree. Draw some leaves on green paper, and cut them out. Snip around their edges to make fronds. Roll up some colored paper to make the tree trunk.

Lots of Eruptions

The red, bubbly "lava" fizzes out of the top of the volcano. The chemical reaction starts as soon as the vinegar mixes with the baking soda. When the volcano has finished erupting, stir inside the bottle with a skewer and pour in some more vinegar. You may get several eruptions this way.

6 Tape round the top and bottom of the trunk, and cut it off square, so it stands up. Tape the palm leaf shapes to the top of the trunk.

7 Using the funnel, carefully pour some of the colored vinegar on to the bicarb in the bottle on the island, and quickly remove the funnel.

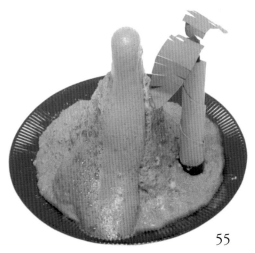

Making Music

Michael Purton

Introduction

What is music? Very simply, music is made from sounds that are pleasing or interesting to hear. Bird songs can be described as music and so can the sounds of the wind or the sea. Many people who write music – composers – have copied the sounds of nature in their music.

Sound is caused by vibrations in the air. The stronger the vibrations, the louder the sound. Musical instruments help us to make music by producing many different sounds. Your own voice is a musical instrument. See how many sounds you can make by altering the shape of your mouth, by using your tongue in different ways, and by changing the pitch of your voice from high to low. We are in fact a mixture of the different types of instruments described below: we are wind instruments because we use air to make sounds; stringed instruments because we speak or sing through our vocal cords, which are like strings low down in our throats; and percussion instruments because we can clap our hands and snap our fingers.

Gabriella's bottle xylophone is a percussion instrument.

Musicians divide musical instruments into different groups:

Percussion Instruments

These are all the instruments that you hit. They were probably the earliest instruments. People from long ago made music by hitting bones together or hitting a hollow tree. Animal skins were stretched over pots or bits of tree trunks to make drums. It is not just drums that are percussion instruments. There are all kinds of fun shakers and rattles which are also used to give rhythm to music.

Claudius has made a bugle which is a wind instrument.

Wind Instruments

These are the instruments that you blow. The air vibrates inside the hollow instrument and makes a sound. The first instruments of this kind were made out of hollow animal horns or bones. Wind instruments sometimes have a "reed" to help make a good sound. A drinking straw works very well for this.

Stringed Instruments

These instruments can be plucked with your fingers or played with a bow. The strings were first made out of hair and silk. All stringed instruments need a hollow box of some kind over which the strings are attached. The box is full of air which vibrates when you play the instrument.

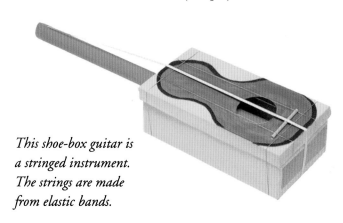

This shoe-box guitar is a stringed instrument. The strings are made from elastic bands.

Jessica is making a drum from a mini-plastic wastebasket.

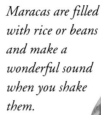

Musical Families

See how many instruments you can think of, and try to place them in a family or group. Is the piano a stringed instrument? It has strings but they are not plucked or played with a bow. If you look inside the piano, you will see that small, felt hammers hit the strings to make the sounds. It is a percussion instrument!

Making Musical Instruments

This chapter will help you to discover lots of different sounds by making your own instruments and then playing them. They are very easy to make. All you need to make music is a cardboard tube or soda can and a few bottle caps or a shower cap! Some of the instruments come from countries like Africa and Latin America, so it is a good chance to decorate them with really bright colors. If you make one of the fun shakers or rattles, it will feel like carnival time!

It's fun to make music with someone else to help.

Maracas are filled with rice or beans and make a wonderful sound when you shake them.

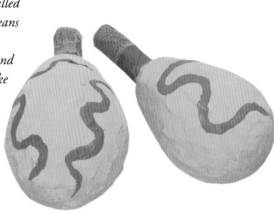

Making Music Together

It is even more fun playing music in groups. Perhaps you and your friends can each make a different instrument to play. First try a rhythm game. Each of you choose a word, and then play the rhythm (the beat) of that word on your instruments over and over again. Try to keep time with everyone else, then experiment by getting louder then softer, and slower then faster.

You could join in with your favorite pop song. Start with the percussion instruments to make the rhythm, then add a wind instrument like a kazoo to sing the tune. See how many different instruments you can use. Make up some music to describe a storm, a ghost story, or a trip to the zoo.

This simple kazoo is made from a cardboard tube and then painted.

Clashing Castanets

Castanets come from Spain, where they are used in flamenco dancing. The dancers stamp their feet and click their castanets in time to the music. It's very exciting to watch them. See if you can dance the same way. Izabella has made her castanets with metal pastry cutters so they make a wonderful sound. *Olé*!

Making music
Clash the pastry cutters together in time to the music. You can also play them by resting your hand on a table.

⚠ Children may need help measuring out, cutting, and scoring the cardboard.

Put your thumb and middle finger through the yellow finger holders, and play away!

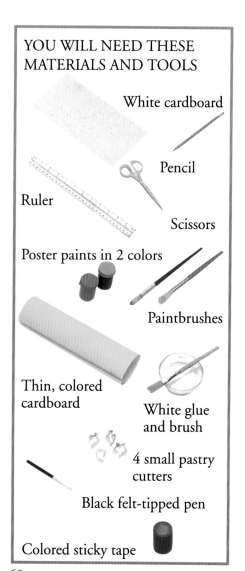

YOU WILL NEED THESE MATERIALS AND TOOLS

White cardboard

Pencil

Ruler

Scissors

Poster paints in 2 colors

Paintbrushes

Thin, colored cardboard

White glue and brush

4 small pastry cutters

Black felt-tipped pen

Colored sticky tape

1 Draw a rectangle 8 in long and 3 in wide on white cardboard. Draw two lines 1 1/2 in apart down the center of the rectangle.

2 Carefully cut out the rectangle. Bend the cardboard along the center lines. It helps if you score along the lines with the ruler first.

3 Paint one side of the cardboard. Allow to dry. Then paint the other side in a different color. Allow to dry while you make the finger holders.

4 Draw four small rectangles on thin cardboard and cut out. Fold around into tubes to fit your middle finger and thumb. Glue together.

5 Decorate one side of the painted cardboard. Draw around the pastry cutters with a black felt-tipped pen to make outline shapes.

6 Reinforce the center where the castanets bend with colored sticky tape. This will make them last longer.

7 Glue the finger holders on to the decorated side of the cardboard. Place them about 1/2 in on each side of the bend. Allow to dry.

8 Glue a pastry cutter to the inside ends of each castanet. Use plenty of glue, and let it dry properly.

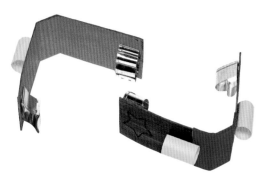

Wastebasket Drum

Drums are very old instruments. They are used for the rhythm in dance music, and they help soldiers to keep in step when they march. Drums were also once used to send signals because you can hear them far away. You can, like Jessica and Alice, play your drum with bare hands or with beaters.

Making music

Do not hit the drum too hard. You will get the best sound if you hit it close to the edge. If you hit different parts of the drum skin, you will get different sounds. Try playing it with a pair of chopsticks or your hands.

A grown-up should cut the cork in half with a craft knife, and push the skewers into the corks to make the beaters. Children may need help with the scissors.

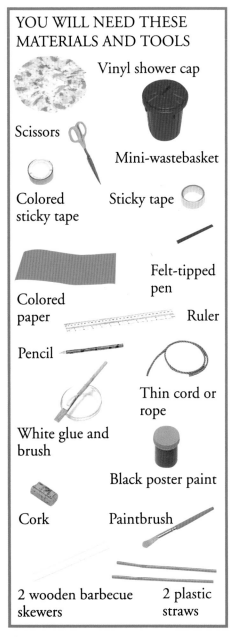

YOU WILL NEED THESE MATERIALS AND TOOLS

Vinyl shower cap

Scissors

Mini-wastebasket

Colored sticky tape

Sticky tape

Colored paper

Felt-tipped pen

Ruler

Pencil

Thin cord or rope

White glue and brush

Black poster paint

Cork

Paintbrush

2 wooden barbecue skewers

2 plastic straws

The finished drum looks very smart.

1 Cut the elastic out of the shower cap. Draw around a plate which is 2 in bigger than the top of the wastebasket. Cut the circle out.

2 Decorate the wastebasket with strips of colored sticky tape.

3 Stretch the plastic circle tightly over the open end of the wastebasket. Stick in place with pieces of sticky tape.

4 Make sure the plastic drum skin is really tight. Then tape right around the edge to hold it in place.

5 Cut a strip of colored paper to fit around the wastebasket top. Make cuts on both sides for a fringe.

6 Glue the fringe around the top of the wastebasket.

7 Tie the cord or rope around the center of the fringe.

8 Ask a grown-up to cut the cork in half across the middle. Paint the corks black. Push the skewers through the straws. Then ask a grown-up to push them into the corks.

Deep Box Bass

Bass instruments play the very lowest notes. This is because they are so large. The large box and the large hole mean there is plenty of space for the air to vibrate and make a deep, booming sound. Nicholas is plucking his box bass with his fingers, like a double-bass player in a jazz band.

Your box bass is all ready for a jazz session!

Making music

Hold the elastic with one hand, and twang it with the other. You can change the sound by pressing the elastic in different places. Thick elastic makes a lower sound than thin elastic.

A grown-up should cut the cork in half with a craft knife. Children may need help with the scissors.

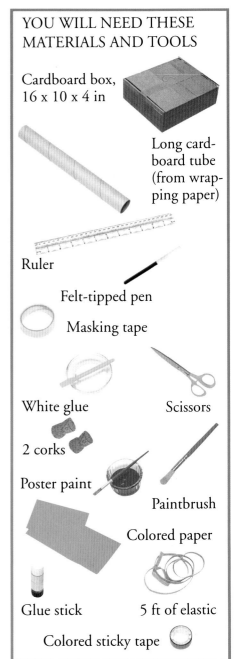

YOU WILL NEED THESE MATERIALS AND TOOLS

Cardboard box, 16 x 10 x 4 in

Long cardboard tube (from wrapping paper)

Ruler

Felt-tipped pen

Masking tape

White glue   Scissors

2 corks

Poster paint   Paintbrush

Colored paper

Glue stick   5 ft of elastic

Colored sticky tape

1 Draw around the cardboard tube to make a circle on the center of the box top. Then draw around the roll of masking tape to make a larger circle on the box front. Position it as shown.

2 Carefully cut out both circles. Pierce the circle with the scissors, and make small cuts out toward the edge of the circle. Then cut around the edge of the circle.

3 Push the tube through the small hole. Glue and tape the tube in place. Ask a grown-up to cut a cork in half. Glue and tape one half, as shown, and the other below the large hole.

4 Paint the box and the tube, and allow to dry.

5 Draw musical notes on the colored paper. Draw around a cork to make the circle shapes.

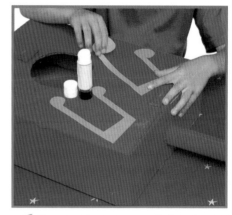

6 Cut out the notes, and glue them on to the front of the box.

7 Ask a grown-up to cut a 3 in slit down the front of the tube. Tie the elastic around the bottom of the tube. Tie a double knot in the other end.

8 Decorate the box with tape. Stretch the elastic down the back of the box and back up the front. Slip the knot into the slit in the tube.

Shoe-box Guitar

The guitar is probably the most popular instrument of all. It's easy to carry, and you can play many different kinds of music on it. Jessica is plucking the elastic string on her guitar, just like a pop star. Electric guitars don't have boxes full of air like this one, so they need electricity to make them sound loud.

Making music

Pluck the elastic string with one hand. With your other hand, press the elastic against the cardboard tube. If you press in different places, you can change the note. Try strumming the string with a coin instead of plucking it.

> ⚠ Children may need help cutting out the circles. See the "Introduction" for an easy way of doing this.

YOU WILL NEED THESE MATERIALS AND TOOLS

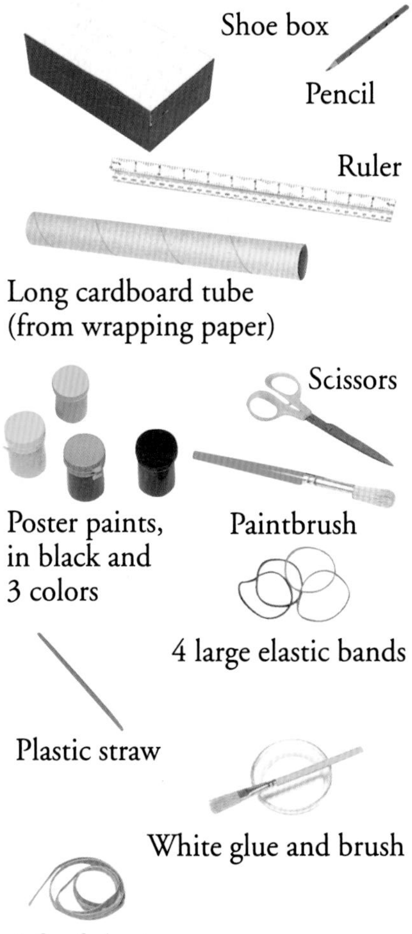

Shoe box

Pencil

Ruler

Long cardboard tube (from wrapping paper)

Scissors

Poster paints, in black and 3 colors

Paintbrush

4 large elastic bands

Plastic straw

White glue and brush

5 ft of elastic

A guitar is a large box full of air. The air vibrates and makes the sound which escapes through the hole.

1 Draw a 4 in circle on the box lid. Draw around the tube on one end of the base of the box. Ask a grown-up to cut out the circles.

2 Draw a guitar shape on the lid of the box. Use a circular shape as a guide, or use a pair of compasses, if you like.

3 Outline the guitar shape in black paint. Fill in with colored paint. Then paint the rest of the box another color. Paint the tube.

4 Stretch two elastic bands across the lid. Position them as shown, just on the edges of the hole.

5 Put the lid on the box. Hold it in place with two more elastic bands. Cut the straw in half. Slide the two pieces under the elastic bands at each end of the guitar. Glue in place.

6 Cut a slit about 3 in long at one end of the tube. Tie a knot in one end of the elastic. Make a loop in the other end, and slide it over the end of the tube.

7 Push the tube into the hole in the box. Stretch the elastic around the back of the box and up around the front. Slip the knot into the slit in the tube.

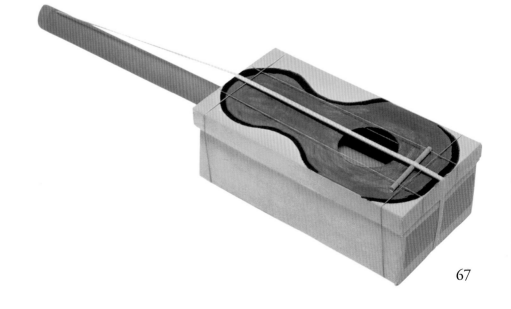

Snakey Maracas

Maracas are played by shaking them in time to music. The rice inside them rattles around to make the sound. Maracas are very popular in Africa and Latin America, where they are often made out of gourds. Nicholas has made his maracas out of papier mâché. This is wet newspaper mixed with glue. When it is dry, it sets hard so that you can paint it.

! Children may need help blowing up and tying the balloons and with cutting the holes in the papier mâché.

When you play your maracas, the snakes will wriggle about and frighten your audience.

Making music

Shake both maracas together in time to the music. You can also play one maraca on its own. Hold it in one hand, and roll it against the palm of your other hand.

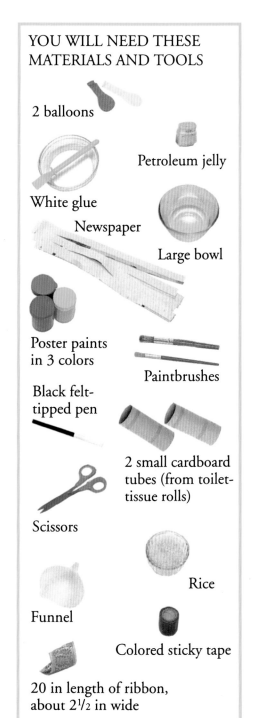

YOU WILL NEED THESE MATERIALS AND TOOLS

2 balloons

Petroleum jelly

White glue

Newspaper

Large bowl

Poster paints in 3 colors

Paintbrushes

Black felt-tipped pen

2 small cardboard tubes (from toilet-tissue rolls)

Scissors

Rice

Funnel

Colored sticky tape

20 in length of ribbon, about 2½ in wide

1 Blow up and tie the balloons. Cover them with petroleum jelly. Support the balloons in jars or mugs, otherwise they will bounce about.

2 Tear the newspaper into strips and squares. Soak them in glue. Cover the balloons with strips. Allow to dry. Then cover them with squares.

3 Wait for the second layer to dry. Then paint the balloons. Allow the paint to dry.

4 Now paint the cardboard tubes, using a different color. Allow the paint to dry.

5 Draw around one of the cardboard tubes on the end of each balloon, and cut out the circles.

6 Spread glue on to one end of each cardboard tube. Push them into the holes in the balloons for handles.

7 Pour the rice into the balloons through the handles. Seal the end of each handle with colored sticky tape. Spread glue on to the handles, then cover them with ribbon.

8 Paint squiggly snakes to decorate the maracas. Use the black felt-tipped pen to draw the snakes' eyes and their forked tongues.

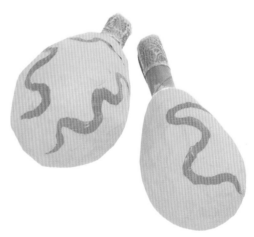

Bottle Xylophone

Bottles make wonderful musical instruments. To get different notes, you add more water. Play the xylophone with different sticks to make different sounds. You can also blow across the top of the bottles. Gabriella has put colored water in her xylophone bottles. This looks pretty, and it also helps her remember the different notes.

Making music

See if you can play a simple tune like "Three Blind Mice." Add a little water to each bottle or pour some out until you get the notes right.

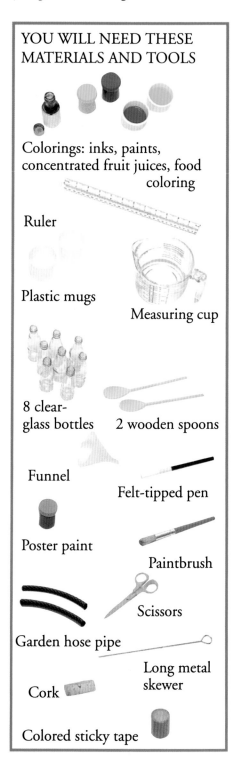

YOU WILL NEED THESE MATERIALS AND TOOLS

Colorings: inks, paints, concentrated fruit juices, food coloring

Ruler

Plastic mugs

Measuring cup

8 clear-glass bottles

2 wooden spoons

Funnel

Felt-tipped pen

Poster paint

Paintbrush

Garden hose pipe

Scissors

Cork

Long metal skewer

Colored sticky tape

A grown-up should push the skewer into the cork. Never leave the colored water in the bottles in case someone is tempted to try a taste. The water is *not* drinkable.

The different sticks make different sounds. What other sticks could you use?

1 Mix seven different colors with water. Use inks, paints, concentrated fruit juices or food coloring.

2 Hit one of the glass bottles with a wooden spoon, and listen to the sound it makes.

3 Mark a line $3/4$ in from the bottom of the bottle. Use a felt-tipped pen.

4 Pour water into the bottle up to the mark. This is much easier if you use a funnel. Hit the bottle again. This time, the sound will be lower.

5 Pour a different-colored water into each bottle. Raise the level of the water by $3/4$ in each time. The bottle with the most water will give the lowest note.

6 Now try blowing across the top of each bottle. This time, the bottle with the most water will give the highest note!

7 Paint the round ends of two wooden spoons. Cover the handles with hose pipe.

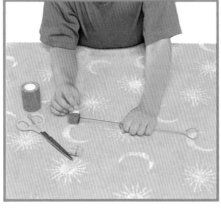

8 Make a different stick. Ask a grown-up to cut the cork in half and push in the skewer. Cover the cork with sticky tape.

Bugle Blow

The first bugles were used to send signals in battle or out hunting. Today, bugles are used in the army to wake everyone up in the morning! The soldier's bugle is a brass instrument but Claudius's bugle is made from garden hose pipe. To get a good sound from this kind of instrument, you need a mouthpiece.

You will need plenty of puff to play your bugle.

Making music

Rest the rim of the mouthpiece on your lips, and take a deep breath. Buzz your lips into the mouthpiece. To play higher notes, blow faster.

⚠ Children may need help cutting and positioning the hose pipe.

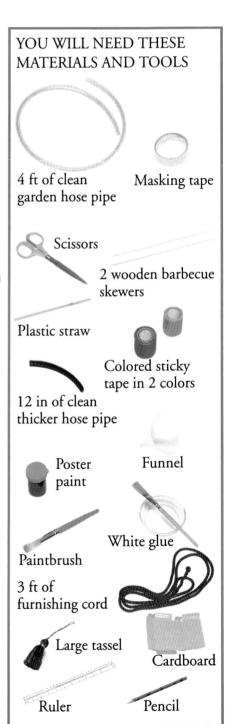

YOU WILL NEED THESE MATERIALS AND TOOLS

4 ft of clean garden hose pipe

Masking tape

Scissors

2 wooden barbecue skewers

Plastic straw

Colored sticky tape in 2 colors

12 in of clean thicker hose pipe

Poster paint

Funnel

White glue

Paintbrush

3 ft of furnishing cord

Large tassel

Cardboard

Ruler

Pencil

1 Bend the thin hose pipe into a circle so that the ends overlap, as shown. Bind the circle together with two pieces of masking tape 3 in apart.

2 Push both skewers into the straw. Place the straw behind the joint in the hose pipe, and tape them together in three places.

3 Cut a piece of thick hose pipe about 6 in long. Slide it on to one end of the hose pipe. Cut a shorter length, and slide it on to the other end.

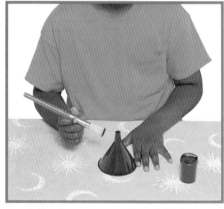

4 Mix the poster paint with the same amount of glue and a little water. Then paint the funnel. Push the funnel into the longer piece of thick hose pipe.

5 Tie the cord on to the bugle so that you can carry it across your chest. Fasten the tassel to the bugle.

6 Measure a square about 5 x 5 in on the cardboard and cut out.

7 Roll the square into a cone shape. Trim off any extra cardboard. Tape the cone together.

8 Fit the cone into the mouthpiece end of the bugle.

Flowerpot Chimes

You do not have to play these wind chimes yourself – if you hang them up the wind will play them for you. The best place to hang them is from a door frame or window frame. Ilaira likes to play her chimes herself, using wooden spoons. The flowerpots are very heavy, so you need a strong coat hanger.

Making music
Hit the flowerpots gently with the spoons. Does the small flowerpot sound different from the large one?

A grown-up should make the holes in the corks and cut them in half with a craft knife. Children may need help with the scissors.

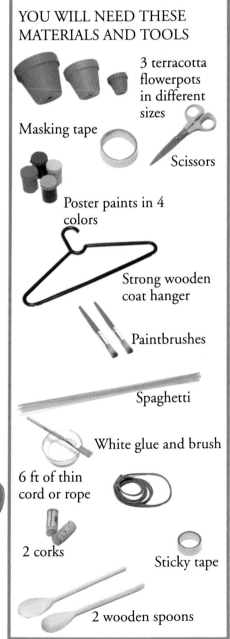

YOU WILL NEED THESE MATERIALS AND TOOLS

3 terracotta flowerpots in different sizes

Masking tape

Scissors

Poster paints in 4 colors

Strong wooden coat hanger

Paintbrushes

Spaghetti

White glue and brush

6 ft of thin cord or rope

2 corks

Sticky tape

2 wooden spoons

The finished flowerpot chimes ready to play a tune. Ilaira has painted her spoons bright green.

1 Use the masking tape to make four triangle shapes on each pot. Paint above the tape in different colors. Allow to dry. Then pull off the tape.

2 Tape along the edge of the painted area. Then paint below the tape in another color. Allow to dry, and remove the tape.

3 Decorate the coat hanger. Use as many colors as possible to make it really bright. Paint the wooden spoons too, if you like.

4 Ask a grown-up to cook some spaghetti. Keep it soft in warm water until you glue it on to the pots. Hold the spaghetti in place with masking tape until the glue dries.

5 Mix the paints together to make brown, and paint the spaghetti. Try not to paint the pots underneath. Allow to dry.

6 Cut the cord into three pieces. Ask a grown-up to make a hole in the corks and cut them in half. Thread a cork on each cord, and tie a knot in one end.

7 Thread the other end of the cord through the hole in the bottom of the flowerpot.

8 Tie each piece of cord to the coat hanger. Tie a good knot. Then bind the cord with sticky tape.

75

Growing Things

Sally Walton and Stephanie Donaldson

Introduction

Gardens and gardeners come in many shapes and sizes. You can be a gardener too, whether you live on a farm with a large garden or in an apartment with some space on a windowsill for a few plants.

Growing things takes time and patience, but the rewards are worth waiting for. There are lots of other things for *Pot marigolds* you to be doing while your seeds are germinating under the soil. Once you see the first green shoots appear you will know that a plant really is going to grow and you are already a gardener!

In this chapter we will show you how to grow lots of different plants yourself, with perhaps just a little help from a grown-up. There are plants that grow very fast and produce something to eat, like mustard and cress. *Strawberries* Some plants take longer to grow but give you special treats, like strawberries. Other plants are grown just for fun, like vegetable tops and a coconut head. So, whether you choose to grow giant sunflowers that take all summer, or sprouting seeds for your salad that are ready in just a few days, you will find out all you need to know by following what the children are doing in the pictures.

Different plants grow, then flower and die with the seasons.

Vegetable tops

Daffodils like the crisp, cold springtime sunshine while nasturtiums thrive in the baking hot summer sun, needing no shade and very little water. Some plants live through the winter, growing new flowers each summer. Others live only for one season but make seeds that will grow into new plants the following year. Houseplants usually come from parts of the world where the weather is warmer all year round, but they grow very happily indoors in countries with cooler climates.

How Plants Begin to Grow

Plants start growing in many different ways and it is important to know how to treat each type. Look at the list below to find out how plants can be grown.

Seeds

A seed needs water to soften its outer shell, and then the new plant sends a root downwards into the soil and a stem upwards, towards the light. The tiniest seeds just need to be scattered on top of the soil, but the larger ones have to be buried. Usually seeds are planted as deep as they are *Seeds* thick. So measure a seed between your fingers and you will know how deep it has to go into the soil in order to grow properly.

Bulbs, corms and tubers

Bulbs

Tubers

Corms

These are thick, fleshy and roundish in shape. A bulb looks like an onion – in fact if you planted an onion it would grow leaves and flowers! They all produce new plants which will grow in the right conditions. Some need icy cold winters underground and others should only be planted when the weather gets warmer. Daffodils grow from bulbs, begonias from corms and dahlias from tubers.

Grow a new plant from a stem cutting

Cuttings

Some plants need very special conditions to make their seeds grow, but you can still grow some new plants from cuttings. Take a piece of a healthy full-grown plant, and stand it in water or soil mix in a warm place. It will grow roots from its stem and you will soon have a strong little plant. Some plants can be grown from leaf or root cuttings as well.

Plantlets

Some fully-grown plants send out long runners which grow miniature plants at their ends. These send down roots of their own if they rest on the soil, and eventually the runners will die back to leave a separate new plant. Strawberries and spider plants grow in this way.

Grow a new plant from plantlets

A Sunflower Race

You have to look up to see a sunflower, because they are the tallest and the biggest flowers that we grow in our gardens. It's great fun to have a sunflower race with your friends or family. Roxy and Dominic are having a sunflower race. Follow the step-by-step photographs to see who won.

Tasty pickings

The flower centers of sunflowers are sometimes as large as dinner plates and packed with tasty seeds. These seeds can be eaten raw once the husks have been removed, or the whole flowerhead can be dried and hung out to feed the birds in winter. In hot countries you can see whole fields of huge sunflowers that are grown to make cooking oil and margarine.

YOU WILL NEED THESE MATERIALS AND TOOLS

Small flowerpots

All-purpose soil mix

Trowel

Sunflower seeds

Plant labels

Watering can

Liquid plant food

Large flowerpots

Long bamboo stakes

1 Fill some pots with soil mix and press in the sunflower seeds.

2 Water the pots and cover them with black plastic, or put them in a dark place to germinate.

Size is Not Everything

If you really love sunflowers but have no space to grow the very tall ones, don't worry – you can grow the smaller types. Buy a packet of sunflower seed called *Helianthus debilis.* Sow the seeds into peat pots and then move them into medium-sized flowerpots or a space in the garden, if you have one. They will grow about 2 ft 8 in tall, and are just as beautiful.

3 When the seeds germinate and you can see a bit of green, move the pots into the light.

4 When the seedlings are big enough to handle, they can be moved into bigger pots. To help them grow strong and tall you will need to give them a liquid feeding once a week. Ask a grown-up to help you with this.

Above: As the plants grow you will need to move them into even larger pots or plant them in the garden. They will need stakes to support them.

Some of the plants will be bigger than you are. Measure each one to find the winner of the great sunflower race. This one is a tie!

Juicy Strawberries

Strawberry plants have very pretty pink or white flowers with yellow centers, and when the petals drop, the fruits begin to grow. They are green at first and then white. As they get bigger and juicier and ripen in the sun, they gradually turn a shiny bright red. If you can bear to wait you will find that the riper they get, the sweeter they taste.

How do baby strawberry plants grow?

Strawberry plants send out long thin stems called runners and baby plants form at their ends. They are fed by the root system of the parent plant through the runner. But if these babies come to rest on soil, they put down roots of their own and no longer need the parent plant to keep them alive. Tania is going to start some baby strawberry plants and grow herself a mouthwatering treat.

Below: Delicious juicy strawberries – well worth waiting for.

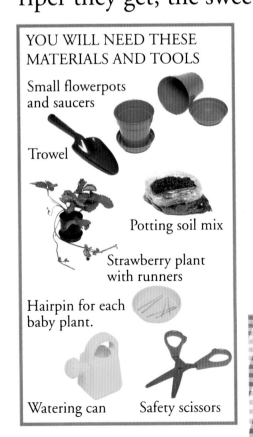

YOU WILL NEED THESE MATERIALS AND TOOLS

Small flowerpots and saucers

Trowel

Potting soil mix

Strawberry plant with runners

Hairpin for each baby plant.

Watering can

Safety scissors

1 Fill the small flowerpots with potting soil mix and gently firm it down.

2 Place your pots around the parent plant so that a baby plant rests in each of the pots. Push a hairpin into the soil mix over the runner.

Cascading Strawberries

If you have only a small space for growing your fruits, a strawberry pot is useful and pretty. It is a tall pot with little "balconies" all the way around it. The idea is to fill the whole pot with soil mix and plant a small strawberry baby in each of the openings. Water each one and plant the biggest strawberry plant in the top of the pot. When the plants begin to grow they will cover the pot and strawberries will hang down in the sun to ripen.

3 Water all the pots. Remember to check the soil mix each day to be sure it never gets too dry.

4 When the plants have rooted you will see tiny new leaves beginning to sprout.

5 If the baby plants feel firm in the soil mix, you can now cut the runners.

6 As your plant grows it will need more space, either in the garden or a larger pot.

7 Remember to water your strawberry plant regularly. If it's kept too dry, the fruit will shrivel.

Coconut Head

This coconut head looks so funny that you'll have to be careful who you show it to – everyone will want one! They are so easy to do, and as the grass grows you will be able to change the hairstyle of your coconut head. You could also try sowing mustard and cress for a really curly hairstyle. Follow the method shown by Dominic and Alex.

Nuts about hair

You can buy grass seed in small amounts from most hardware stores or garden centers, and just 2 oz will grow a really good "head of hair" for your coconut. You will have to ask a grown-up to saw or break the top off your coconut, because the shells are really hard. If you haven't eaten fresh coconut before or drunk coconut milk, try some – it's really tasty! Put some out for the birds as a treat.

YOU WILL NEED THESE
MATERIALS AND TOOLS

Fresh coconut

Flowerpot

Marker

Trowel

Soil mix

Grass seed

Soil sieve

Watering can

Black plastic bag

1 Ask a grown-up to take the top off your coconut. Pour out the milk and ask someone to help you remove the flesh – it's quite difficult.

2 Stand the coconut shell in a flower-pot to keep it from falling over, and draw a face on it with a thick, black marker.

3 Fill your coconut with soil mix, pressing it down gently.

4 Scatter grass seed thickly over the top of the soil mix.

5 Sieve a thin layer of soil mix over to cover all the seed. Press down gently again.

6 Water and cover with a black plastic bag, or put in a dark place until the seeds have begun to grow.

7 When green shoots appear, stand the coconut in the light and water when it looks dry. When the grass has grown over the rim of the coconut, it is ready for its first haircut.

Above: Before and after! If you keep snipping the grass as it grows, it will get thicker and thicker!

Jolly Geraniums

Geraniums are lovely, bright flowering plants that live outside in the sunny weather. In the winter they can be brought inside to live on a sunny windowsill. Their flowers are either red, white or pink and they have pretty shaped leaves – some of them are scented. Rub a leaf between your fingers to discover their surprising smells of rose, lemon, pineapple or peppermint!

Taking a cutting

The best way to grow your very own geranium plant is to find somebody who owns a nice bushy geranium, and ask them to take a cutting for you. Tania is going to start a plant from a cutting. Just follow the step-by-step instructions, and you will be able to grow one too.

YOU WILL NEED THESE MATERIALS AND TOOLS

3–5 in long stem cutting from geranium

Small flowerpot lined with a plastic bag

Trowel or scoop

Seed and cutting soil mix

String

Plant labels

1 Ask a grown-up to take a cutting from a non-flowering shoot of a big geranium plant. Cut the stem just below a node or leaf joint.

2 Take off all leaves except for the small ones at the top.

3 Line a small pot with a plastic bag and fill with moist (but not wet) soil mix. Seed and cutting soil mix is the best type to use.

4 Make a hole in the soil mix for your cutting with a finger. Put the cutting in the hole. Press the soil mix down gently around the cutting to hold it in place.

5 Lift the edges of the plastic bag, gather it up and tie it around the stem of the cutting with string. Take care not to damage the stem by tying it too tightly.

6 Fold the top of the bag back down over the pot, write a label for your plant and place your pot on a light, but not too sunny, windowsill. After ten days your cutting should have rooted. When it has grown new leaves, lift up the plastic bag and you will see new roots in the soil mix. You can now remove the bag and plant the geranium in a larger pot.

Above: What an achievement. Your very own plant from a cutting.

Lazy Summer Afternoons

Nasturtiums and pot marigolds are two plants for lazy gardeners! They need very little care – in fact they thrive and produce more flowers in poor-quality soil. So don't pamper them – they just don't like it. Follow the steps shown in the photographs to find out how it's done.

Pretty useful

Nasturtium flowers range from yellow to deep red, and marigold flowers are bright orange or yellow. Nasturtium flowers can be eaten raw. They have a peppery taste, and some supermarkets sell packets of the flowers that would turn a plain salad into a party dish. Marigolds are not eaten but they are used to make soothing skin lotions and healing ointments. Their petals were once used to color cheeses, custards and cakes, too.

Neither of these plants likes to have its roots disturbed, so Dominic and Roxy are starting them off in little peat pots. The plants can be potted in these because the peat will gradually dissolve into the new soil mix.

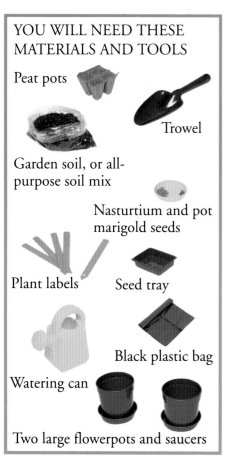

YOU WILL NEED THESE MATERIALS AND TOOLS

Peat pots

Trowel

Garden soil, or all-purpose soil mix

Nasturtium and pot marigold seeds

Plant labels

Seed tray

Black plastic bag

Watering can

Two large flowerpots and saucers

1 Fill the little peat pots with garden soil or soil mix.

2 Either sow one nasturtium or two marigold seeds in each pot, and gently press them in.

3 Write a label for each kind of flower and put it in the pot.

4 Stand the pots in a seed tray and water them until the pots turn dark brown all over.

5 Cover the pots with a black plastic bag until the seeds have germinated and you can see green shoots. Then move them into a light place.

6 When the seeds are 2–3 in tall they can be planted in bigger pots. Break off each peat pot, and plant the pot with the seedlings.

7 Both marigolds and nasturtiums will produce seeds on their flower-heads when the petals have dropped. Let these dry and save them in labeled packets for next year's flower crop.

Above and right: The orange-yellow color of marigold and nasturtium flowers are especially summery. You could transfer your plants to a windowbox for a pretty outdoor display of color.

Crazy-Shaped Mustard and Cress

Once you have learned how to grow mustard and cress, you can make all sorts of shapes and patterns with your plants. Try animals and faces, or even your own name. Mustard and cress are fun to grow and delicious to eat in salads and sandwiches.

How to grow mustard and cress

Mustard and cress are two of the easiest and quickest plants you can grow. They don't need flowerpots or soil mix, just cotton balls and water. Sprinkle the seeds onto damp cotton balls and water them each day – as Alex and Reece are doing here. Within a week the little plants will be growing strongly and one week after that you can harvest them with a pair of scissors and then eat them. Your mustard and cress will taste just as good as the type you can buy from the store.

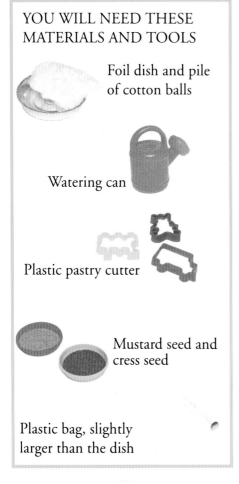

YOU WILL NEED THESE
MATERIALS AND TOOLS

Foil dish and pile
of cotton balls

Watering can

Plastic pastry cutter

Mustard seed and
cress seed

Plastic bag, slightly
larger than the dish

1 Line a foil dish with a layer of cotton balls.

2 Pour on water, until all the cotton is damp.

3 Place the plastic pastry cutter in the center of the dish.

4 Very carefully, scatter mustard seeds inside the cutter.

5 Now scatter the cress seeds all around the rest of the dish.

Mustard and Cress "Eggheads"

You can grow mustard and cress in eggshells. Save the shell from your boiled egg and line it with damp cotton balls. Sow the seed thickly and wait for your "egghead" to grow its hair. Use markers to draw a happy face on the shell, and trim the mustard and cress into a nice "hairstyle".

6 Place the dish in the plastic bag and put it in a dark place. Check the dish each day to see if the seeds have germinated. When they have, remove the plastic bag and place the dish on a light windowsill.

7 Add a little water to the dish each day – just enough to keep the cotton wet. When the plants are as tall as your little finger, you can cut the mustard and cress and put them in a salad or sandwich.

Chocolate-Pot Plant

Can you believe your nose? This lovely plant smells exactly like chocolate! It is a very special sort of cosmos daisy that is bought as a small plant and, if it is kept out of the cold, it will flower again next year.

What a wonderful smell!

To make the smell of chocolate even stronger and more delicious, Dominic and Alex have used a special mulch to cover the soil. This mulch is made from cocoa shells after the cocoa beans have been removed to make chocolate. It has a lovely chocolate smell and is also good for the soil!

YOU WILL NEED THESE MATERIALS AND TOOLS

Large clay pot

Acrylic paint

Paintbrush

Crocks

Cosmos daisy *(Cosmos astrosanguineus)*

All-purpose soil mix

Trowel

Saucer filled with gravel

Cocoa-shell mulch

Watering can

Right: A chocolate-pot plant would be a lovely and unusual present for someone special – if you can bear to part with it.

1 Use a round paintbrush to paint colored dots all around your flowerpot.

2 When the paint has dried, put some crocks in the bottom, so that the drainage hole does not clog up.

3 Remove your plant from its pot very carefully. If its roots have started to curl around inside the pot, gently loosen the roots as Alex is doing here.

4 Put the plant into the decorated pot and fill all around the roots with soil mix, pressing down the edges until the plant is firmly in position.

5 Cover the bare soil around the plant with a thick layer of cocoa-shell mulch.

6 Stand the pot on the saucer filled with gravel and water the plant thoroughly.

7 Press the flower petals gently between your fingers to release a delicious chocolate smell.

8 After all that hard work, and the tempting smells, a real chocolate was irresistible.

More Surprising Smells

A lemon balm plant will grow very quickly. Plant it in a medium-sized flowerpot in all-purpose soil mix. When you rub the leaves between your fingers, a lovely lemony smell is released. Another surprising plant is one of the sages, *Salvia elegans*. It has a mouthwatering smell of pineapple. There is a mint and a geranium that have a pineapple smell too.

93

Index

Acknowledgments

The publishers would like to thank the following children for appearing in this book, and of course their parents: Josie and Lawrence Ainscombe, Rosie Anness, Joshua and Tania Ayshford, Rebecca Clee, Dean Denning, Benjamin Ferguson, Kirsty and Rebecca Fraser, Liam and Lorenzo Green, Alexandra and Oliver Hall, Reece Harle, Karina Kelly, Nicholas Lie, Alex and Otis Lindblom-Smith, Gabriella and Izabella Malewska, Ilaira and Joshua Mallalieu, Alexander Martin-Simons, Alice and Jessica Moxley, Tania Murphy, Dominic Paneth, Alice Purton, Brandon Rayment, Antonino Sipiano, Roxy Walton, George Wheeler, Claudius Wilson, Andreas Wiseman.

Gratitude also to Hampden Gurney School, the Walnut Tree Walk Primary School and St. John the Baptist C. of E. School.

Contributors: Stephanie Donaldson, Sarah Maxwell, Steve and Jane Parker Michael Purton, Sally Walton.